NOW YOU CAN READ. . . . .
THE MIRACLE ON THE MOUNTAIN

STORY RETOLD BY ARLENE C. ROURKE

ILLUSTRATED BY GWEN GREEN

Library of Congress Cataloging in Publication Data

Rourke, Arlene, 1944-
    The miracle on the mountain.

    Summary: A brief retelling of the life of Jesus,
concluding with his Transfiguration on the mountain
before his three favorite Apostles.
    1. Jesus Christ—Transfiguration—Juvenile literature.
2. Jesus Christ—Biography—Public life—Juvenile
literature. [1. Jesus Christ—Biography. 2. Jesus Christ—
Transfiguration] I. Title.
BT410.R68 1985   232.9'56   85-20489
ISBN 0-86625-319-X

GROLIER ENTERPRISES CORP.

NOW YOU CAN READ....

THE MIRACLE ON THE MOUNTAIN

Jesus grew up in Nazareth. His
mother, Mary, and Joseph watched
Him over the years. He grew in
strength and wisdom. When He
reached manhood, He knew that He
must begin His mission. His work
was to teach people to do right and
love God. Only then, would they be
happy with God forever.

Jesus left Nazareth and went to the Jordan River. He knew that His cousin, John, was preaching there. John was known as John the Baptist. He would baptize people in the river to cleanse them of their sins. Then, they could start life anew.

Jesus went to John and asked to be baptized. John was surprised that the Son of God would want to be baptized by him. But, he did as Jesus asked. After He had been baptized, Jesus thanked John and went on His way. This was the beginning of His life as a teacher.

At first, Jesus travelled the countryside alone. He would stop at a place and begin talking to people. He was strong and gentle.

His words had great wisdom. People were drawn to Him. Before long, a large crowd would gather around Him, listening to His every word.

Jesus chose twelve men to help Him carry out His work. They came to be known as the Apostles. After His death, the Apostles would spread His word to many lands and convert many people.

The first Apostle was Simon. Jesus named him "Peter." Peter means "rock."

"On this rock I will build my church," Jesus said.

Peter's brother, Andrew, went with him. Two other fishermen, John and his brother, James, followed.

Philip and Bartholomew were added.

Matthew, the tax collector, came next.

He was followed by James the Little and his brother, Jude.

Thomas, known as "doubting Thomas," and another Simon came later.

Finally, there was Judas Iscariot.
Judas was the Apostle who would betray Jesus to His enemies for thirty pieces of silver.
But, that would be in the future.

Now, Jesus was just beginning His work.

Jesus and His Apostles travelled from town to town preaching the word of God. Sometimes Jesus would heal the sick. Sometimes He would just sit and talk quietly with people.

One day, Jesus gathered His Apostles around Him.

"Who do the people think I am?" Jesus asked.

"They think you are a prophet," answered Philip.

"Yes," said James. "They think you are one of the great prophets who has been reborn. Some say you are John the Baptist. Since his death, his followers are sure he will come back to life."

"I have heard some people say that you are the prophet Elijah returning again," said Andrew.

Jesus was silent for a moment. "Who do you think I am?" He asked finally.

The Apostles looked at Him in amazement.

"Why, you are the Saviour, the Son of God," Peter blurted out.

"My friends, the people still do not understand our work. We are going to have some hard times in the future. Some people will turn against us. Some people will even betray us," with that Jesus looked at Judas. Judas did not understand.

Jesus went on. "Some day I will not be here with you."

"But, you will not let any harm come to you. You are all powerful," said Peter.

"Your faith must be strong." Jesus went on. "When I am gone, you will need it. You must carry on our work."

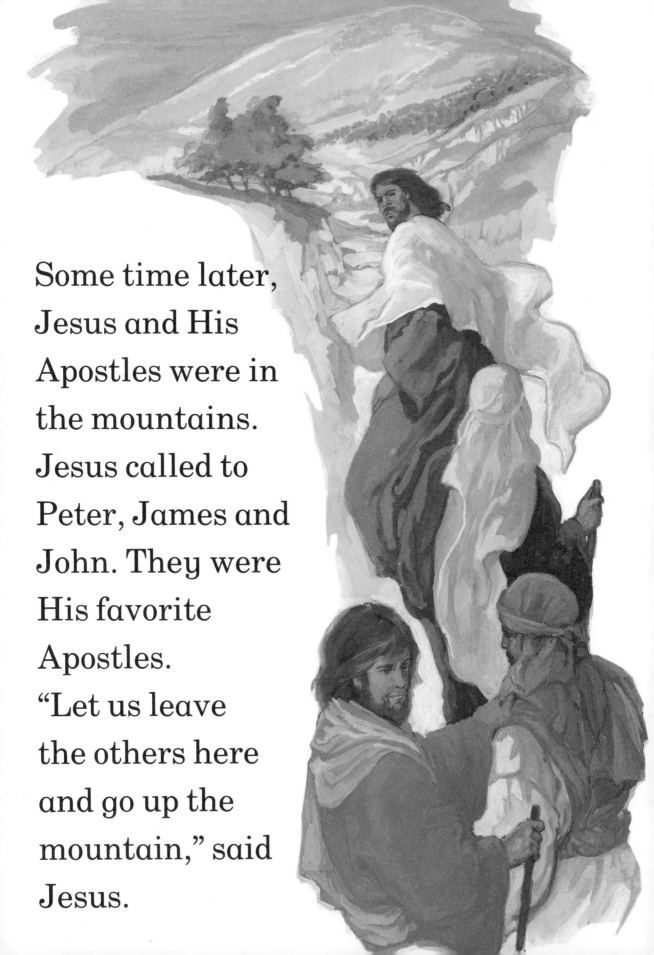

Some time later, Jesus and His Apostles were in the mountains. Jesus called to Peter, James and John. They were His favorite Apostles. "Let us leave the others here and go up the mountain," said Jesus.

While the others waited below, the four men climbed to the top of the mountain.

It grew colder and colder. Every so often, one of the Apostles would look down the mountain. They were very high up. Their friends were so far away. Still, Jesus walked on and on.

They climbed through the clouds. They
could see the sun. It was so bright!
The Apostles stopped. Jesus climbed
to the very top of the mountain.
The figure of Jesus stood out against
the sun and the clouds. It was a
beautiful vision. The Apostles were
almost blinded by the light. Then,
they saw that Jesus was not alone.

Two other men stood there with him. One was Moses and the other was Elijah. They both bowed to Jesus.

Peter, James and John stood without moving. They were amazed. Suddenly, the vision disappeared.

The blinding light was gone. Jesus came toward them, and spoke. "What you have seen you must not tell to anyone. When I am no longer with you, remember this. Your faith will be strong."

Silently, He led them down the mountain. Peter, James and John never forgot what they saw that day.

All these appear in the pages of the story. Can you find them?

Andrew

James and John

Peter

Judas

Jesus

Now tell the story in your own words.